# Christmas carols, new and old

Henry Ramsden Bramley, John Stainer

**Nabu Public Domain Reprints:**

You are holding a reproduction of an original work published before 1923 that is in the public domain in the United States of America, and possibly other countries. You may freely copy and distribute this work as no entity (individual or corporate) has a copyright on the body of the work. This book may contain prior copyright references, and library stamps (as most of these works were scanned from library copies). These have been scanned and retained as part of the historical artifact.

This book may have occasional imperfections such as missing or blurred pages, poor pictures, errant marks, etc. that were either part of the original artifact, or were introduced by the scanning process. We believe this work is culturally important, and despite the imperfections, have elected to bring it back into print as part of our continuing commitment to the preservation of printed works worldwide. We appreciate your understanding of the imperfections in the preservation process, and hope you enjoy this valuable book.

*FIRST SERIES.*

# Christmas Carols

## NEW AND OLD

THE WORDS EDITED BY THE

Rev. HENRY RAMSDEN BRAMLEY, M.A.,

FELLOW AND TUTOR OF SAINT MARY MAGDALEN COLLEGE, OXFORD.

THE MUSIC EDITED BY

SIR JOHN STAINER, M.A., MUS. DOC.,

OF THE SAME COLLEGE.

---

*Price, in paper cover, 1s.; cloth gilt, 2s.*
First, Second, and Third Series, cloth gilt, 4s.
Words complete, paper cover, 4d.; cloth, 6d.; each Series, 1½d.

---

LONDON: NOVELLO AND COMPANY, LIMITED.
NEW YORK: THE H. W. GRAY CO., SOLE AGENTS FOR THE U.S.A.

LONDON:
NOVELLO AND COMPANY, LIMITED,
PRINTERS

For Verses 2, 3.

2. Never fell melodies half so sweet As those which are filling the skies; And never a palace shone half so fair As the manger bed where our Saviour lies; No night in the year is half so dear As this which has ended our sighs.

3 Now a new Power has come on the earth,
   A match for the armies of Hell:
A Child is born who shall conquer the foe,
   And all the spirits of wickedness quell;
For Mary's Son is the Mighty One
   Whom the prophets of God foretell.

side, Christ Jesus our Saviour was born on this tide.

2 At Bethlehem city in Jewry it was
That Joseph and Mary together did pass,
All for to be taxed with many one moe,
Great Cæsar commanded the same should be so.
                          Aye and therefore, &c.

3 But when they had entered the city so fair,
A number of people so mighty was there,
That Joseph and Mary, whose substance was small,
Could find in the inn there no lodging at all.
                          Aye and therefore, &c.

4 Then were they constrained in a stable to lie,
Where horses and asses they used for to tie:
Their lodging so simple they took it no scorn,
But against the next morning our Saviour was born.
                          Aye and therefore, &c.

5 The King of all kings to this world being brought,
Small store of fine linen to wrap Him was sought;
But when she had swaddled her young Son so sweet,
Within an ox manger she laid Him to sleep.
                          Aye and therefore, &c.

6 Then God sent an angel from Heaven so high,
To certain poor shepherds in fields where they lie,
And bade them no longer in sorrow to stay,
Because that our Saviour was born on this day.
                          Aye and therefore, &c.

7 Then presently after the shepherds did spy
Vast numbers of angels to stand in the sky;
They joyfully talkèd and sweetly did sing,
To God be all glory, our heavenly King.
                          Aye and therefore, &c.

8 To teach us humility all this was done,
And learn we from thence haughty pride for to shun:
A manger His cradle who came from above,
The great God of mercy, of peace, and of love.
                          Aye and therefore, &c.

2.

Come, ye poor, no pomp of station
   Robes the Child your hearts adore:
He, the Lord of all salvation,
   Shares your want, is weak and poor:
Oxen, round about behold them;
   Rafters naked, cold, and bare,
See the shepherds, God has told them
   That the Prince of Life lies there.

3.

Come, ye children, blithe and merry,
   This one Child your model make;
Christmas holly, leaf, and berry,
   All be prized for His dear sake;
Come, ye gentle hearts, and tender,
   Come, ye spirits, keen and bold;
All in all your homage render,
   Weak and mighty, young and old.

4.

High above a star is shining,
   And the Wisemen haste from far:
Come, glad hearts, and spirits pining:
   For you all has risen the star.
Let us bring our poor oblations,
   Thanks and love and faith and praise:
Come, ye people, come, ye nations,
   All in all draw nigh to gaze.

5.

Hark! the Heaven of heavens is ringing
   "Christ the Lord to man is born!"
Are not all our hearts too singing,
   "Welcome, welcome, Christmas morn?"
Still the Child, all power possessing,
   Smiles as through the ages past;
And the song of Christmas blessing,
   Sweetly sinks to rest at last.

## 5. Come, tune your heart.

1. Come, tune your heart, To bear its part, And ce-le-

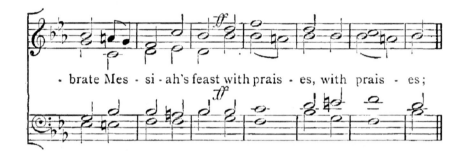

-brate Mes-si-ah's feast with prais-es, with prais-es;

Let love in-spire The joy-ful choir, While to the

God of Love glad hymns it rais-es, it rais-es.

2.

Exalt His Name;
With joy proclaim,
God loved the world, and through His Son forgave us;
Oh! what are we,
That, Lord, we see
Thy wondrous love, in Christ who died to save us!

3.

Your refuge place
In His free grace,
Trust in His Name, and day by day repent you;
Ye mock God's Word,
Who call Him Lord,
And follow not the pattern He hath lent you.

4.

O Christ, to prove
For Thee my love,
In brethren Thee my hands shall clothe and cherish;
To each sad heart
Sweet Hope impart,
When worn with care, with sorrow nigh to perish.

5.

Come, praise the Lord;
In Heaven are stored
Rich gifts for those who here His Name esteemèd;
Alleluia,
Alleluia;
Rejoice in Christ, and praise Him, ye redeemèd.

2.

They looked up and saw a Star,
Shining in the East, beyond them far,
And to the earth it gave great light,
And so it continued both day and night.
                Nowell, &c.

3.

And by the light of that same Star,
Three Wisemen came from country far;
To seek for a King was their intent,
And to follow the Star wherever it went.
                Nowell, &c.

4.

This Star drew nigh to the north-west,
O'er Bethlehem it took its rest,
And there it did both stop and stay,
Right over the place where Jesus lay.
                Nowell, &c.

5.

Then entered in those Wisemen three,
Full reverently upon their knee,
And offered there, in His Presence,
Their gold, and myrrh, and frankincense.
                Nowell, &c.

6.

Then let us all with one accord,
Sing praises to our Heavenly Lord,
That hath made Heaven and earth of nought,
And with His Blood mankind hath bought.
                Nowell, &c.

7 Jesu, hail! O God most holy.

(14)

2.

To enrich my desolation,
To redeem me from damnation,
Wrapt in swathing-bands Thou liest,
Thou in want and weakness sighest:
     Might transcending, &c

3.

Low abased, where brutes are sleeping,
God's belovèd Son is weeping;
Judge supreme, true Godhead sharing,
Sinner's likeness for us wearing!
     Might transcending, &c.

4.

Jesu, Thine my heart is solely,
Draw it, take it to Thee wholly:
With Thy sacred Fire illume me,
Let it inwardly consume me.
     Might transcending, &c.

5.

Hence let idle fancies vanish,
Hence all evil passions banish;
Make me like Thyself in meekness,
Bind to Thee my human weakness.
     Might transcending, &c.

# 8 Good Christian men, rejoice.

1. Good Chris-tian men, re-joice .. With heart, and soul, and

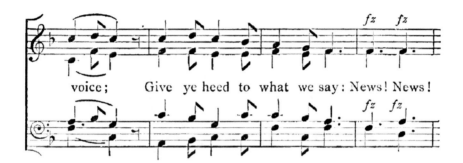

voice; Give ye heed to what we say: News! News!

Je-sus Christ is born to-day: Ox and ass be-

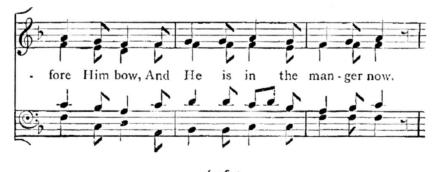

-fore Him bow, And He is in the man-ger now.

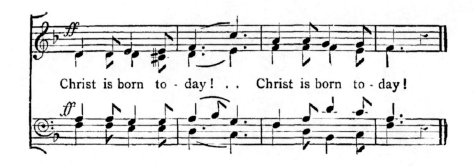

Christ is born to-day! .. Christ is born to-day!

2.

Good Christian men, rejoice
With heart, and soul, and voice;
  Now ye hear of endless bliss:
    Joy! Joy!
  Jesus Christ was born for this!
He hath oped the heav'nly door,
And man is blessed evermore.
  Christ was born for this!

3.

Good Christian men, rejoice
With heart, and soul, and voice;
  Now ye need not fear the grave:
    Peace! Peace!
  Jesus Christ was born to save!
Calls you one and calls you all,
To gain His everlasting hall:
  Christ was born to save!

## Sleep, Holy Babe!

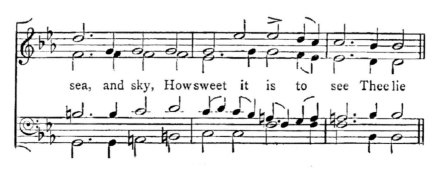

2.

Sleep, holy Babe! Thine Angels watch around,
  All bending low with folded wings,
  Before the Incarnate King of kings,
In reverent awe profound.

3.

Sleep, Holy Babe! while I with Mary gaze
  In joy upon that Face awhile,
  Upon the loving infant smile
Which there divinely plays.

4.

Sleep, holy Babe! ah! take Thy brief repose;
  Too quickly will Thy slumbers break,
  And Thou to lengthened pains awake,
That Death alone shall close.

### 2.

*Tenor Solo.* "Hither, page, and stand by me.
　　　　If thou know'st it, telling,
　　Yonder peasant, who is he?
　　　　Where and what his dwelling?"
*Treble Solo.* "Sire, he lives a good league hence,
　　　　Underneath the mountain;
　　Right against the forest fence,
　　　　By Saint Agnes' fountain."

### 3.

*Tenor Solo.* "Bring me flesh, and bring me wine,
　　　　Bring me pine-logs hither;
　　Thou and I will see him dine,
　　　　When we bear them thither."
*Chorus.* Page and monarch forth they went,
　　　　Forth they went together;
　　Through the rude wind's wild lament
　　　　And the bitter weather.

### 4.

*Treble Solo.* "Sire, the night is darker now,
　　　　And the wind blows stronger;
　　Fails my heart, I know not how,
　　　　I can go no longer."
*Tenor Solo.* "Mark my footsteps, good my page!
　　　　Tread thou in them boldly:
　　Thou shalt find the winter's rage
　　　　Freeze thy blood less coldly."

### 5.

*Chorus.* In his master's steps he trod,
　　　　Where the snow lay dinted;
　　Heat was in the very sod
　　　　Which the saint had printed.
　　Therefore, Christian men, be sure,
　　　　Wealth or rank possessing,
　　Ye who now will bless the poor,
　　　　Shall yourselves find blessing.

## 11 When I view the Mother holding.

1. When I view the Mother holding In her arms the heavenly Boy, . . Thousand blissful thoughts unfolding, Melt my heart with sweetest joy, with sweetest joy. . . . . . .

2.

The next good joy that Mary had,
  It was the joy of two;
To see her own Son Jesus Christ
  Making the lame to go.
Making the lame to go, Good Lord;
  And happy, &c.

3.

The next good joy that Mary had,
  It was the joy of three;
To see her own Son Jesus Christ
  Making the blind to see.
Making the blind to see, Good Lord;
  And happy, &c.

4.

The next good joy that Mary had,
  It was the joy of four;
To see her own Son Jesus Christ
  Reading the Bible o'er.
Reading the Bible o'er, Good Lord;
  And happy, &c.

5.

The next good joy that Mary had,
  It was the joy of five;
To see her own Son Jesus Christ
  Raising the dead to life.
Raising the dead to life, Good Lord;
  And happy, &c.

6.

The next good joy that Mary had,
  It was the joy of six,
To see her own Son Jesus Christ
  Upon the Crucifix
Upon the Crucifix, Good Lord;
  And happy, &c.

7.

The next good joy that Mary had
  It was the joy of seven;
To see her own Son Jesus Christ
  Ascending into Heaven.
Ascending into Heaven, Good Lord;
  And happy, &c.

## 13 On the Birthday of the Lord.

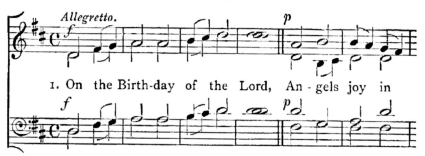

1. On the Birth-day of the Lord, An-gels joy in

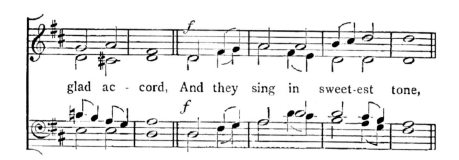

glad ac-cord, And they sing in sweet-est tone,

Glo-ry be to God a-lone, Glo-ry be to

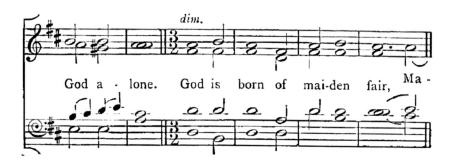

God a-lone. God is born of mai-den fair, Ma-

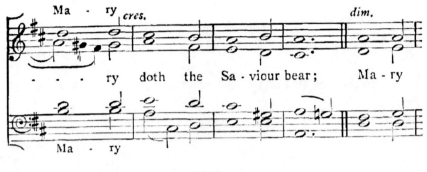

2.

These good news an Angel told
To the shepherds by their fold,
Told them of the Saviour's Birth,
Told them of the joy for earth.
      God is born, &c.

3.

Born is now Emmanuel,
He, announced by Gabriel,
He, Whom Prophets old attest,
Cometh from His Father's Breast.
      God is born, &c.

4.

Born to-day is Christ the Child,
Born of Mary undefiled,
Born the King and Lord we own;
Glory be to God alone.
      God is born, &c.

2.

Why lies He in such mean estate,
   Where ox and ass are feeding?
Good Christian, fear: for sinners here
   The silent Word is pleading:
Nails, spear, shall pierce Him through,
   The Cross be borne, for me, for you:
Hail, hail, the Word made flesh,
   The Babe, the Son of Mary!

3.

So bring Him incense, gold, and myrrh,
   Come peasant, King to own Him;
The King of kings, salvation brings;
   Let loving hearts enthrone Him.
Raise, raise, the song on high,
   The Virgin sings her lullaby:
Joy, joy, for Christ is born,
   The Babe, the Son of Mary!

## 15 Glorious, beauteous, golden-bright.

Glorious, beauteous, golden-bright,
Shedding softest, purest light,
Shone the stars that Christmas night;
When the Jewish shepherds kept
Watch beside their flocks that slept.

2.
But the stars' sweet golden gleam
Faded quickly as a dream,
'Mid the wondrous glory-stream,
That illumined all the earth,
When Christ's angels sang His birth.

4.

But that light no more availed,
All its splendour straightway paled
In His light whom angels hailed:
Even as the stars of old,
'Mid the brightness lost their gold.

5.

Now no more on Christmas night,
Is the sky with angels bright,
But for ever shines the Light;
Even He whose birth they told
To the shepherds by the fold.

## 16 Waken! Christian children.

1. Waken! Christian children, Up and let us sing, With glad voice, the praises Of our new-born King.

2. Up! 'tis meet to welcome,
   With a joyous lay,
   Christ, the King of Glory,
   Born for us to-day.

3. Come, nor fear to seek Him,
   Children though we be;
   Once He said of children,
   "Let them come to Me."

4. In a manger lowly,
   Sleeps the Heavenly Child;
   O'er Him fondly bendeth
   Mary, Mother mild.

5. Far above that stable,
   Up in Heaven so high,
   One bright star out-shineth,
   Watching silently.

6. Fear not then to enter,
   Though we cannot bring
   Gold, or myrrh, or incense
   Fitting for a King.

7. Gifts He asketh richer,
   Offerings costlier still,
   Yet may Christian children
   Bring them if they will.

8. Brighter than all jewels
   Shines the modest eye;
   Best of gifts He loveth
   Infant purity.

9. Haste we then to welcome,
   With a joyous lay,
   Christ, the King of Glory,
   Born for us to-day.

## 17. A Child this day is born.

1. A Child this day is born, A Child of high renown; Most worthy of a sceptre, A sceptre and a crown.

CHORUS.
Glad tidings to all men, Glad tidings sing we may, Because the King of

(38)

kings . . . . . Was born on Christ-mas-Day.

2.

These tidings shepherds heard
   Whilst watching o'er their fold;
'Twas by an Angel unto them
   That night revealed and told.
      Glad tidings, &c.

3.

Then was there with the Angel
   An host incontinent*
Of heavenly bright soldiers,
   All from the highest sent.
      Glad tidings, &c.

4.

They praised the Lord our God
   And our celestial King:
All glory be in Paradise,
   This heavenly host do sing.
      Glad tidings, &c.

5.

All glory be to God,
   That sitteth still on high,
With praises and with triumph great,
   And joyful melody.
      Glad tidings, &c.

---

* Immediately.

## 18. Carol for Christmas-Eve.

1. Listen, lordings, unto me, a tale I will you tell;
Which, as on this night of glee, in David's town befel.
Joseph came from Nazareth, with Mary, that sweet maid:
Weary were they, nigh to death; and for a lodging pray'd. Sing high, sing high, sing low, sing low, sing high, sing low, sing

2.

In the inn they found no room; a scanty bed they made:
Soon a Babe from Mary's womb was in the manger laid.
Forth He came as light through glass; He came to save us all.
In the stable ox and ass before their Maker fall.
     Sing high, sing low, &c.

3.

Shepherds lay afield that night, to keep the silly sheep,
Hosts of Angels in their sight came down from heaven's high steep.
Tidings! tidings! unto you: to you a Child is born,
Purer than the drops of dew, and brighter than the morn.
     Sing high, sing low, &c.

4.

Onward then the Angels sped, the shepherds onward went,
God was in His manger bed, in worship low they bent.
In the morning, see ye mind, my masters one and all,
At the Altar Him to find who lay within the stall.
     Sing high, sing low, &c.

## 19 When Christ was born of Mary free.

1. When Christ was born of Mary free, In Bethlehem that fair citie, Angels sang there with mirth and glee, "In excelsis Gloria,

CHORUS.
In excelsis Gloria, In excelsis Gloria,

2.

Herdsmen beheld these Angels bright,
To them appearing with great light,
Who said God's Son is born to-night.
    "In excelsis Gloria."

3.

The King is come to save mankind,
As in Scripture truths we find,
Therefore this song we have in mind,
    "In excelsis Gloria."

4.

Then, dear Lord, for Thy great grace,
Grant us in bliss to see Thy face,
That we may sing to Thy solace,
    "In excelsis Gloria."

## 20. 'Twas in the Winter cold.

### A CHRISTMAS MORNING HYMN.

1. 'Twas in the win-ter cold, when earth Was de-so-late and wild, .. That an-gels welcomed at His birth The ev-er-last-ing Child. From realms of ev-er-bright'ning day, And from His throne a-bove He

came, with hu-man kind to stay, All low-li-ness and love.

2 Then in the manger the poor beast
   Was present with his Lord;
Then swains and pilgrims from the East
   Saw, wondered, and adored.
And I this morn would come with them
   This blessed sight to see,
And to the Babe of Bethlehem
   Bend low the reverent knee.

3 But I have not, it makes me sigh,
   One offering in my power;
'Tis winter all with me, and I
   Have neither fruit nor flower.
O God, O Brother, let me give
   My worthless self to Thee;
And that the years which I may live
   May pure and spotless be:

4 Grant me Thyself, O Saviour kind,
   The Spirit undefiled,
That I may be in heart and mind
   As gentle as a child;
That I may tread life's arduous ways
   As Thou Thyself hast trod,
And in the might of prayer and praise
   Keep ever close to God.

5 Light of the everlasting morn,
   Deep through my spirit shine;
There let Thy presence newly born
   Make all my being Thine:
There try me as the silver, try,
   And cleanse my soul with care,
Till Thou art able to descry
   Thy faultless image there.

# INDEX.—First Series

| No. | Title. | Source of Words. | Air. | Page |
|---|---|---|---|---|
| I. | God rest you merry, Gentlemen | Traditional | Traditional | 2 |
| II. | The Manger Throne | W. C. Dix | C. Steggall, Mus. Doc. | 4 |
| III. | A Virgin unspotted | Traditional | Traditional | 6 |
| IV. | Come, ye lofty | The Rev. Archer Gurney | Sir George J. Elvey, Mus. Doc. | 8 |
| V. | Come, tune your heart | Translated from the German by Frances Elizabeth Cox | The Rev. Sir Fred. A. G. Ouseley, Bart., M.A., Mus. Doc. | 10 |
| VI. | The first Nowell | Traditional | Traditional | 12 |
| VII. | Jesu, hail! | Translated from the Latin by the Rev. H. R. Bramley | J. Stainer | 14 |
| VIII. | Good Christian men, rejoice | The Rev. Dr. Neale | Old German | 16 |
| IX. | Sleep, holy Babe | The Rev. E. Caswall | The Rev. J. B. Dykes, Mus. Doc. | 18 |
| X. | Good King Wenceslas | The Rev. Dr. Neale | Helmore's Christmas Carols | 20 |
| XI. | When I view the Mother holding | Translated from the Latin by the Rev. H. R. Bramley | J. Barnby | 22 |
| XII. | The seven joys of Mary | Traditional | Traditional | 28 |
| XIII. | On the Birthday of the Lord | Translated from the Latin by the Rev. R. F. Littledale, LL.D. | The Rev. J. B. Dykes, Mus. Doc. | 30 |
| XIV. | What Child is this? | W. C. Dix | Old English | 32 |
| XV. | Glorious, beauteous, golden-bright | Anna M. E. Nichols | Maria Tiddeman | 34 |
| XVI. | Waken, Christian children | The Rev. S. C. Hamerton, M.A. | The Rev. S. C. Hamerton, M.A. | 37 |
| XVII. | A Child this day is born | Traditional | Traditional | 38 |
| XVIII. | Carol for Christmas Eve | The Rev. H. R. Bramley | The Rev. Sir Fred. A. G. Ouseley, Bart. | 40 |
| XIX. | When Christ was born | Harleian MS. | Arthur H. Brown | 42 |
| XX. | Christmas Morning Hymn | The Rev. C. J. Black | J. Barnby | 44 |

CPSIA information can be obtained at www.ICGtesting.com
Printed in the USA
LVOW11s1451111213

364879LV00010B/426/P